GW01368203

- These student worksheets are intended to act alongside the corresponding revision guide to help reinforce your understanding and improve your confidence.

- Every worksheet is cross-referenced to "G.C.S.E. PHYSICAL EDUCATION" edited by Peter Urwin and Donna Sheppard.

- The questions concentrate purely on the content you need to cover, and the limited space forces you to choose your answer carefully.

> These worksheets can be used ...
>
> ... as <u>classwork sheets</u> where pupils use their revision guide to provide the answers ...
>
> ... as <u>harder classwork sheets</u> where pupils study the topic first, then answer the questions without their guides ...
>
> ... as easy to mark <u>homework sheets</u> which test understanding and reinforce learning ...
>
> ... as the basis for <u>learning homeworks</u> which are then tested in subsequent lessons ...
>
> ... as <u>test material</u> for topics ...
>
> ... as a <u>structured revision programme</u> prior to the exams.

- Remember to fill in your score at the bottom of each page in the small grey box , and also to put your score in the 'marks' column on the contents page.

CONTENTS

Score   Page No.

The Human Body

4   Health And Fitness
5   The Skeleton
6   The Vertebral Column
7   Types Of Joint
8   Movements Of Joints
9   Muscles
10   How Muscles Work
11   The Components Of The Circulatory System
12   The Blood Vessels And Blood
13   Monitoring The Circulation
14   The Breathing System
15   Breathing And Capacity For Gas Exchange
16   Energy From Food
17   Respiration 1 - Aerobic
18   Respiration 2 - Anaerobic
19   The Nervous And Hormonal Systems
20   Energy Requirements
21   Diet And Nutrition
22   Special Diets

Training And Exercise

23   Reasons For Exercise
24   The Principles Of Training
25   Muscular Endurance And Strength
26   Muscular Strength
27   Speed
28   Flexibility 1
29   Flexibility 2
30   Aerobic And Anaerobic Training
31   Specific Training Methods 1
32   Specific Training Methods 2
33   Specific Training Methods 3
34   Training Requirements For Sport
35   Long Term Effects Of Training
36   The Body's Response To Exercise
37   Temperature Regulation And Water Balance
38   Fitness Testing
39   Testing Specific Fitness

Aspects Of Sport

40   Prevention Of Injury
41   Footwear For Sport
42   Playing Safe
43   Personal Hygiene
44   Posture

CONTENTS

Score   Page No.

Aspects Of Sport (Cont.)

45   Safety Aspects 1 - DR ABC Procedure
46   Safety Aspects 2 - Mouth To Mouth Resuscitation
47   Safety Aspects 3 - Cardiac Massage
48   Safety Aspects 4 - R.I.C.E. Treatment
49   Safety Aspects 5 - Injuries Requiring Hospital Treatment
50   Safety Aspects 6 - Other Injuries and Ailments
51   Factors Affecting Performance 1 - Introduction
52   Factors Affecting Performance 2 - Environment, Pressure, Disability, illness
53   Factors Affecting Performance 3 - Somatotype
54   Factors Affecting Performance 4 - Gender, Age, Lifestyle
55   Factors Affecting Performance 5 - Personality And Mindset
56   Factors Affecting Performance 6 - Substance Abuse
57   Factors Affecting Performance 7 - Acquisition Of Skill
58   Factors Affecting Performance 8 - Feedback
59   Technology In Sport

Issues In Sport

60   Sponsorship 1
61   Sponsorship 2
62   The Media And Sport 1
63   The Media And Sport 2
64   Sporting Behaviour
65   Amateur And Professional Sport
66   Facilities And Providers
67   How A Sports Club Works
68   Funding For Sport
69   International Sport 1
70   International Sport 2
71   International Sport 3

Participation In Sport

72   The Role Of The School In Promoting Participation
73   Changing Attitudes 1 - Social Change
74   Changing Attitudes 2 - Women And The Disabled
75   Changing Attitudes 3 - Encouraging Participation
76   Modes Of Participation
77   Factors Affecting Participation
78   Types Of Competition
79   Leisure Time
80   Provision For Excellence 1
81   Provision For Excellence 2
82   The Framework, Structure And Organisation Of Sport In The U.K.
83   Organisations Influencing Participation 1
84   Organisations Influencing Participation 2

1. Each of the following sentences relate to either Health or Fitness.
   Circle the initial to indicate which you think it is.

When I finish school I have enough energy to go to netball training.	H / F
When I finish school I can go home and have something to eat.	H / F
If I lose at football I am disappointed, but I realise it is only a game, and I don't over-react.	H / F
I am not ill, nor do I have any injuries.	H / F
I do not get so tired during lessons that I can't concentrate.	H / F
After I have finished my Saturday job I still have enough energy to go out with my friends.	H / F
If I need help or advice I can rely on my friends or family.	H / F

2. General Fitness or Health Related Fitness, has five components.

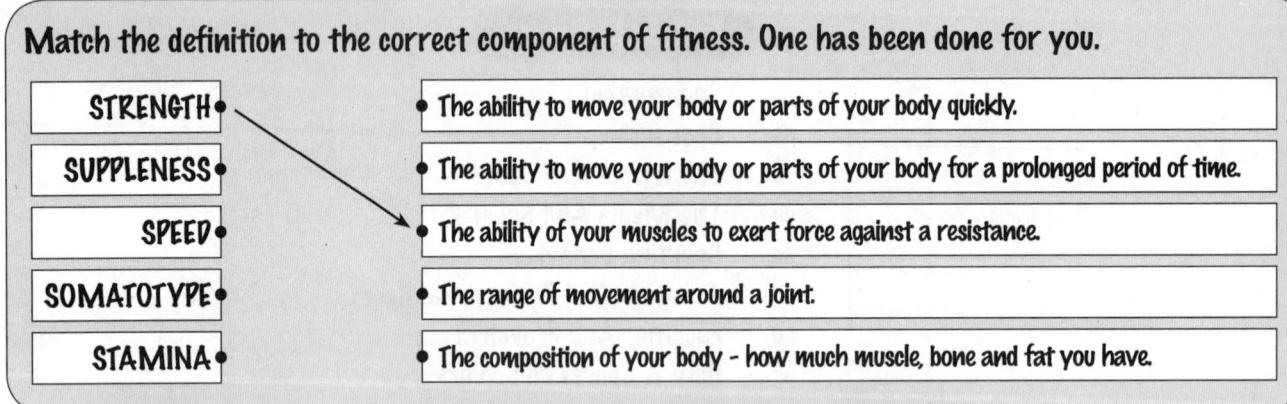

Match the definition to the correct component of fitness. One has been done for you.

STRENGTH • → The ability to move your body or parts of your body quickly.

SUPPLENESS • The ability to move your body or parts of your body for a prolonged period of time.

SPEED • The ability of your muscles to exert force against a resistance.

SOMATOTYPE • The range of movement around a joint.

STAMINA • The composition of your body - how much muscle, bone and fat you have.

3. Can you think which types of motor fitness are most important for the sports below?
   Remember, each sports person's fitness will be made up of different components of motor fitness
   e.g. a hurdler will need excellent 'agility' and 'balance.'

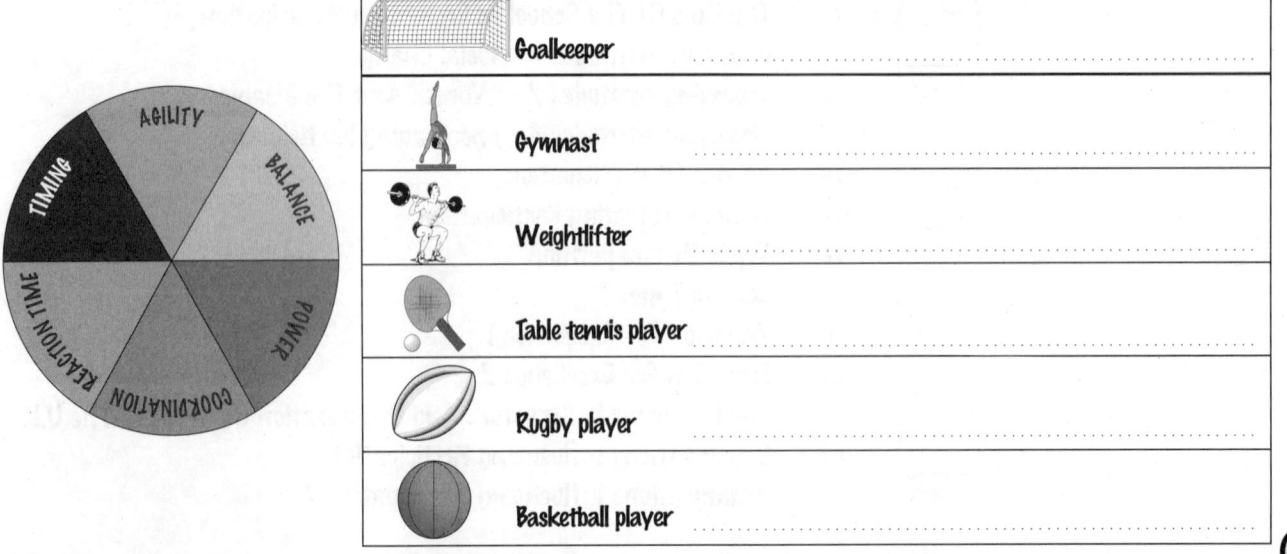

Goalkeeper ....

Gymnast ....

Weightlifter ....

Table tennis player ....

Rugby player ....

Basketball player ....

1. Complete the crossword below using the clues in the list.

ACROSS

1. Longest bone in the body. (5)
3. Makes up part of your hips. (6)
6. Takes place inside the long bones. (5,10)
7. Type of bone found in the cranium and pelvis. (4)
9. Function of the skeleton that gives the body shape and holds vital organs in place. (7)
11. Type of bone found in the vertebral column. (9)
15. There are 206 of these in the body. (5)
16. Type of long bones. (9)
17. Your funny bone. (7)
19. Also known as your collar bone. (8)

DOWN

1. The thinner of the two bones in your lower leg. (6)
2. The thicker of the two bones in your lower arm. (6)
3. It is not attached to any other bone. (7)
4. Also known as your shoulder blade. (7)
5. Bones held together by freely moveable joints facilitate this. (8)
8. Your shin bone. (5)
9. Ribs attach to this bone. (7)
10. Protects the brain. (7)
12. The femur is an example of this type of bone. (4)
13. These bones help protect the heart. (4)
14. The type of bone found in the hands and feet. (5)
18. Thinner of the two bones found in the lower arm. (4)

1. a) The vertebral column is divided into five sections. Below is a description of each section and the letters to form each descriptive word. Rearrange the letters to reveal their names.

The ribs attach to these vertebrae	CCOTRHAI
Fused vertebrae known as your tail bone.	CYXCOC
These neck vertebrae allow your neck to bend.	VERLICCA
These are the largest vertebrae and endure great stress when walking or running.	ARMLBU
These fused vertebrae form part of the pelvic girdle.	RASCAL

b) Which vital part of the body is protected by the vertebral column?

2. a) Explain what a ligament is.

Ligament →

b) Describe TWO functions of cartilage within a joint.

i)

ii)

c) Friction in a joint is reduced by cartilage and a special fluid. Name the special fluid and state where it is produced.

3. What is the function of the discs between the vertebrae?

1. a) There are THREE types of joint. Name them.

i) _____   ii) _____   iii) _____

b) Give an example of each.

i) _____   ii) _____   iii) _____

c) Describe some characteristics of each joint.

i) _____   ii) _____   iii) _____

2. a) Label this diagram of a freely moveable joint.

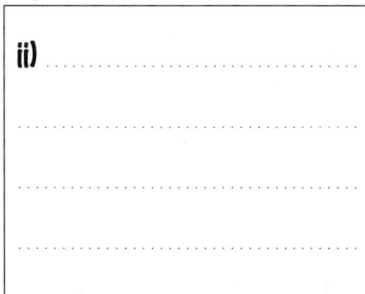

b) Another word for a freely moveable joint is a _____ **joint.**

3. Complete the table, which describes different types of freely moveable joints.

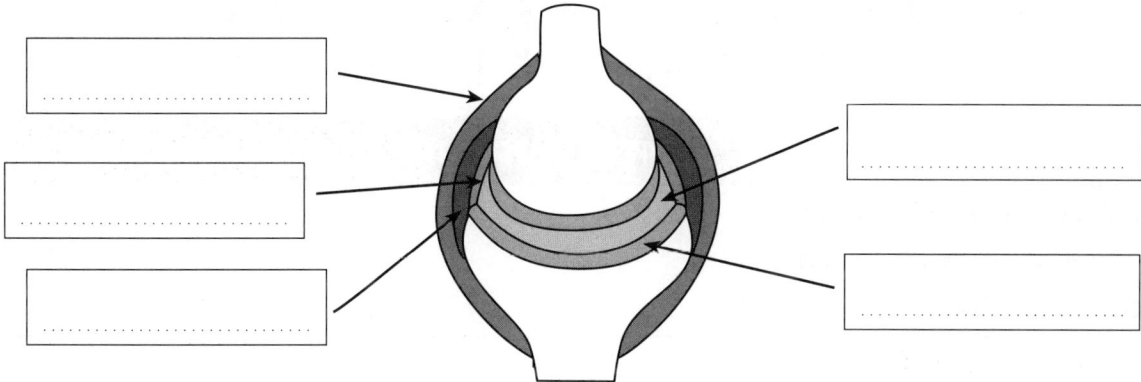

NAME	TYPE OF MOVEMENT	EXAMPLE
		Neck
Saddle		
	Full range	
		Knee
Gliding		
		Wrist

1. Find the names of the various types of movement and the joints which can perform them, in the wordsearch below, and then match them to their correct definitions.

E	B	Y	A	E	Q	O	R	S	U	M	D	B	M	F
N	O	I	X	E	L	F	G	E	C	X	S	A	E	E
R	O	R	F	K	J	L	M	S	A	D	D	L	E	P
I	P	I	V	O	T	E	R	C	L	B	R	L	I	L
J	E	T	T	I	A	X	V	K	A	D	H	A	E	N
A	B	D	U	C	T	I	O	N	U	E	G	N	I	H
P	A	C	D	B	U	D	I	F	E	G	O	D	T	E
O	D	I	O	L	Y	D	N	O	C	L	G	S	W	K
E	D	O	I	C	K	R	M	R	A	C	G	O	S	J
R	U	A	T	N	F	E	P	U	M	R	N	C	V	L
L	C	R	E	W	B	R	G	D	C	D	I	K	A	G
D	T	S	N	O	I	T	A	T	O	R	D	E	H	B
D	I	P	U	R	C	U	Z	G	N	S	I	T	D	B
A	O	S	E	A	T	N	Y	E	X	L	L	C	A	S
S	N	O	I	S	N	E	T	X	E	E	G	O	O	N

	TYPE OF MOVEMENT	JOINTS WHICH CAN PERFORM ON THEM
A joint bent or FLEXED, so that one of the bones of the joint moves towards the other.		
A joint straightened or EXTENDED in its natural position to its full extent.		
A movement AWAY from the central line of the body.		
A movement which causes part of the body to describe a complete circle.		
A turning movement around a central point or pivot.		
A movement TOWARDS the central line of the body.		

1. Name the THREE types of muscle and give an example of each.

2. Name a muscle group that creates:

a) Abduction

b) Adduction

c) Rotation

Name THREE muscle groups that create:

d) Flexion

i)

ii)

iii)

e) Extension

i)

ii)

iii)

3. a) Use the following words to label the diagram below.

| BICEP | ORIGIN | TENDON | TRICEP | INSERTION | SCAPULA | HUMERUS |

b) Define the term origin:

c) Define the term insertion:

d) Explain why the origin moves towards the insertion during a muscular contraction.

1. Complete the following crossword.

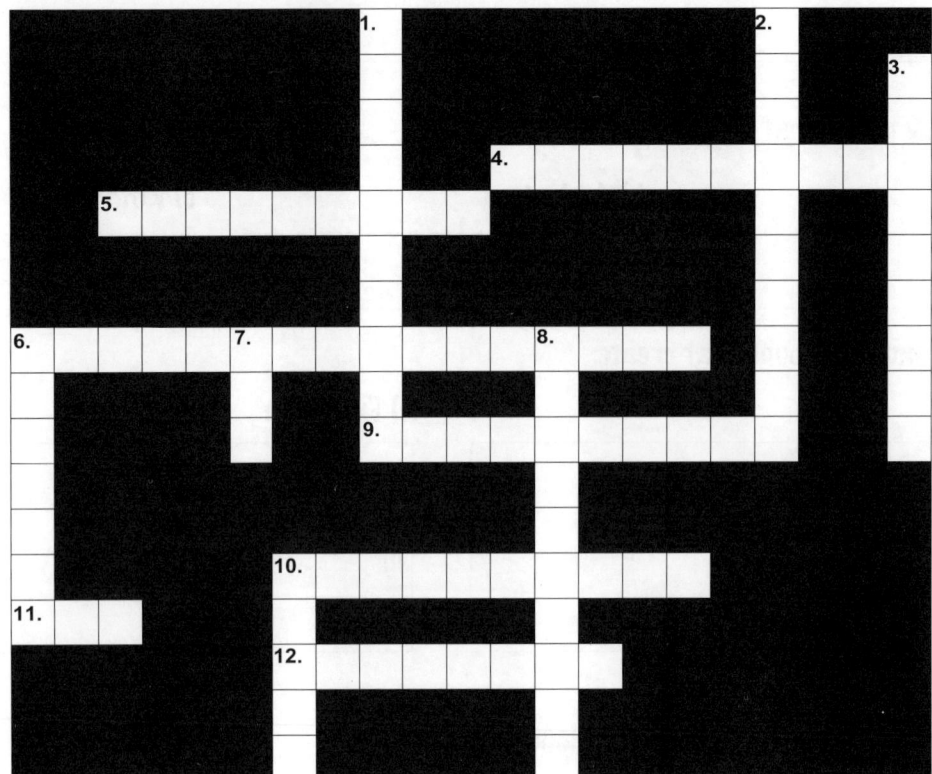

ACROSS

4. A muscular contraction in which a muscle is shortening under tension. (10)

5. A muscular contraction during which a muscle stays the same. (9)

6. Muscles working in opposition to each other are said to be working .... (16)

9. The type of muscle fibre used during endurance events. (4, 6)

10. The muscle responsible for most of the work during a movement. (5,5)

11. The minimum number of muscles around a joint. (3)

12. A type of contraction in which the muscle changes its length. (8)

DOWN

1. Muscles working to assist the prime mover are called .... (10)

2. Muscle fibres that are used during fast power events. (4, 6)

3. Muscles lengthening under tension are said to be making an .... contraction. (9)

6. An alternative word for describing the prime mover. (7)

7. The number of directions in which a muscle can create movement. (3)

8. The name given to the muscle that relaxes in order to allow movement at a joint. (10)

10. In order to create movement in two directions at a joint, muscles need to work in .... (5)

1. a) The circulatory system has THREE main components. Name them.

i) ....

ii) ....

iii) ....

b) Blood pumped from the heart to the body transports two substances, needed for energy. Name them.

i) ....

ii) ....

c) What does blood remove from the cells of the body?

....

2. a) Match the number on the diagram to the component of the circulatory system.

b) Indicate with a tick the type of blood each component carries. The lungs and capillaries carry both and have been done for you.

c) Indicate on the diagram the direction of blood flow, using arrows. ➡➡➡ ➡➡➡

NUMBER	COMPONENT	OXYGENATED ➡	DEOXYGENATED ➡
	Aorta		
	Right side of heart		
	Capillaries in the lungs	✓	✓
	Vena Cava		
	Left side of heart		
	Capillaries in the body	✓	✓
	Pulmonary vein		
	Pulmonary artery		

3. The heart acts as a pump in a double circulatory system. Explain this statement.

....

....

....

....

....

....

....

1. a) There are THREE types of blood vessel. Name them.

i) ....

ii) ....

iii) ....

b) Give TWO characteristics of each vessel.

i)

i)

i)

ii)

ii)

ii)

2. EXCHANGE OF SUBSTANCES takes place in the capillaries. Explain this term using the diagram below.

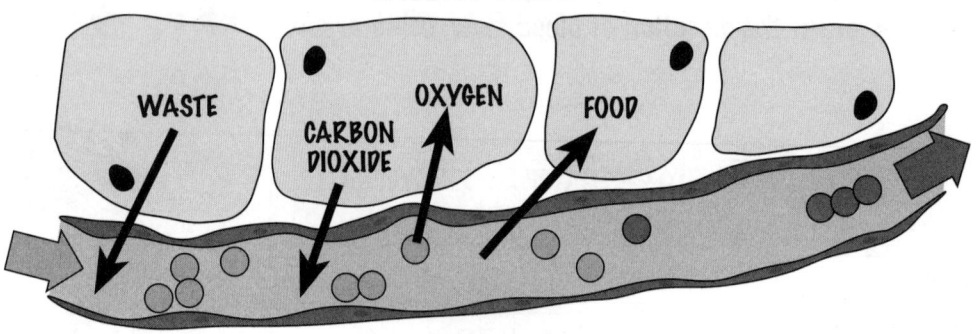

MUSCLE CELLS

WASTE CARBON DIOXIDE OXYGEN FOOD

A CAPILLARY VESSEL
(one cell thick)

3. a) Your blood consists of FOUR components. Name them.

i) ....

ii) ....

iii) ....

iv) ....

b) Give TWO characteristics of each component.

i)

i)

i)

i)

ii)

ii)

ii)

ii)

1. a) The average pulse of an adult is 72 b.p.m. What is a pulse?

b) What does a pulse give a clear indication of?

2. a) Explain why an increase in heart rate produces an increased cardiac output.

b) During exercise your cardiac output needs to increase.
   Explain this statement using the following words to construct your answer.

(INCREASED ENERGY DEMANDS)   (OXYGEN)   (CARBON DIOXIDE)

(PULSE)   (STROKE VOLUME)   (FOOD)

c) Calculate the cardiac output of a heart which has a stroke volume of 70cm³ and a heart rate of 70 b.p.m.

d) Calculate the stroke volume of a heart which has a heart rate of 140 b.p.m. and a cardiac output of 10,500cm³/min.

1. a) Label the diagram below.

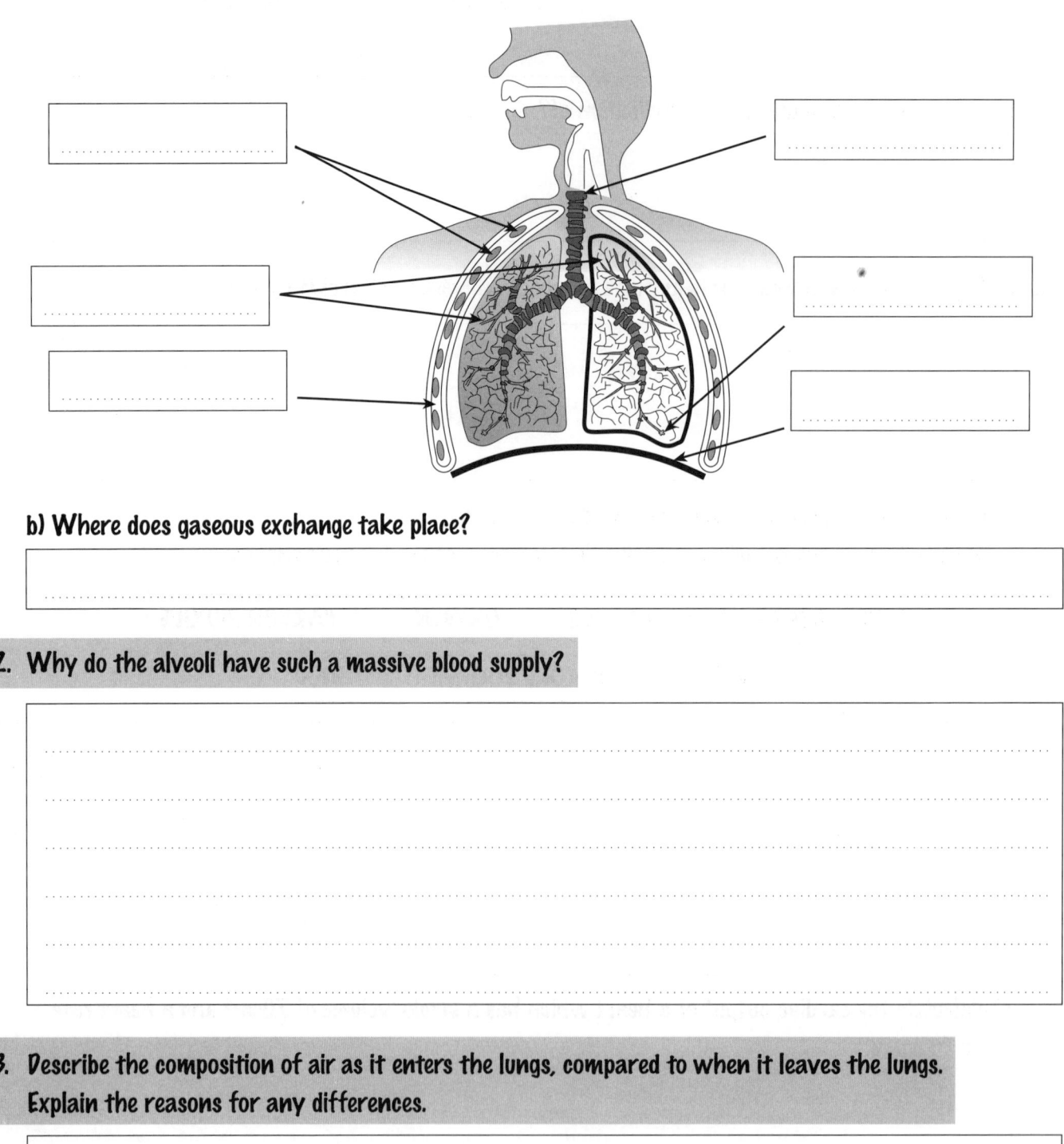

b) Where does gaseous exchange take place?

2. Why do the alveoli have such a massive blood supply?

3. Describe the composition of air as it enters the lungs, compared to when it leaves the lungs. Explain the reasons for any differences.

1. Use the following words to help describe how air is drawn into the lungs during inhalation.

(INTERCOSTAL MUSCLES) (INCREASE IN VOLUME) (CONTRACT)

(THORAX) (DIAPHRAGM) (DECREASE IN PRESSURE)

2. Use the following words to help describe how air is forced out of the lungs during exhalation.

(INTERCOSTAL MUSCLES) (RELAX) (INCREASE IN PRESSURE)

(DIAPHRAGM) (DECREASE IN VOLUME) (THORAX)

3. Define the following terms:

a) Tidal volume

b) Respiratory rate

c) Minute volume

4. Calculate the minute volume when the tidal volume is 2.5 litres and the respiratory rate is 20 breaths/minute.

1. Humans use energy from food for a variety of tasks, including maintenance of temperature, reproduction, excretion and feeding. Name THREE other ways of using energy from food.

i) ....

ii) ....

iii) ....

2. Briefly explain the importance of each energy use, within a sporting context.

i) ....
....

ii) ....
....

iii) ....
....

3. a) How is starch used as a food source?

....
....
....
....

b) The starch we eat is converted into a different substance in order to enter the blood. What is this substance called?

....
....

c) Glucose in the blood is used in THREE different sites, name them.

i) ....

ii) ....

iii) ....

d) What use is made of the glucose at each site?

i) ....
....

ii) ....
....

iii) ....
....

1. Write out the word equation for aerobic respiration.

2. a) The three products of the cellular combustion of glucose and oxygen are carbon dioxide, water and energy. Describe what happens to each product.

   i) CO_2

   ii) H_2O

   iii) Energy

   b) State ONE advantage of aerobic respiration.

   ✓

   c) State ONE disadvantage of aerobic respiration.

   ✗

3. The maximum amount of energy your body can produce aerobically is determined by how much oxygen your body can make available to the cells.

   a) Explain how endurance athletes manage to do this very efficiently.

   b) When does aerobic respiration normally occur?

1. a) Write out the word equation for anaerobic respiration.

....

b) When does your body produce energy anaerobically?

....

c) Why can't a person produce energy anaerobically over a prolonged period of time?

....

2. a) What is an oxygen debt?

....

b) Why does a sprinter continue to breathe heavily for several minutes after finishing a race?

....

3. a) State ONE advantage of anaerobic respiration.

✔ ....

b) State ONE disadvantage of anaerobic respiration.

✗ ....

4. a) How much energy is produced in anaerobic respiration compared to aerobic respiration?

....

b) How much faster is this energy produced?

....

1. a) What are the nervous and hormonal systems?

....

b) i) What does the nervous system allow us to do?

....

ii) Explain how it does this

....

c) Briefly describe, in your own words, how the hormonal system works.

....
....
....

2. What part does the brain play in the body's communication system?

....

3. Explain, in detail, how and why a damaged spinal cord would affect a person's ability to move.

....
....
....

4. a) What is the effect of adrenalin on the body?

....

b) Give TWO instances when the body might produce adrenalin.

i) ....   ii) ....

5. a) Describe what your body's response might be when you eat a bar of chocolate.

....
....

b) What do you think the effect of your body not producing insulin might be? Explain your answer.

....
....

1. a) Why is a person's total energy requirement always greater than their working energy?

b) Describe THREE factors which will affect a person's total energy requirements.

i)

ii)

iii)

2. A person had a Basal Metabolic Rate (BMR) of 1000 Kilocalories and a working energy of 1500 Kilocalories. Explain fully the effect, on their body, of consuming 2000 Kilocalories of food.

3. Describe some of the problems associated with:

i) Obesity

ii) Anorexia

1. The following table lists a variety of foods and their various components. Complete the table by placing a tick in the corresponding columns to indicate which nutrients are found in each food.

The first two have been done for you as examples.

| Food Type | COMPONENTS | | | | | | | | |
| | | | | Vitamins | | | Minerals | | |
	Carbohydrate	Fat	Protein	A	C	D	Iron	Calcium	Fibre
MILK	✓	✓	✓	✓		✓		✓	
CABBAGE	✓				✓		✓		✓
POTATOES									
CHICKEN									
TUNA FISH									
ORANGES									
BANANA									
BACON									
PASTA									
CRISPS									
CHOCOLATE									
CAKE									
BROCCOLI									
TOMATOES									

2. a) Describe THREE problems you might encounter if you had an unbalanced diet.

i) ....

ii) ....

iii) ....

b) Why does having buttered toast for breakfast not constitute a healthy start?
   Which nutritional component is missing from the meal?

....

....

....

1. a) Divide the plate to indicate the proportions of the three main components which are needed in a balanced meal.

   b) Shade in the boxes to give your diagram a key.

   ☐ Carbohydrate

   ☐ Protein

   ☐ Fat

2. Describe the diet of a weightlifter and a marathon runner, in order to highlight the differences between the two. Give examples of particular food types that might play an important role in each athlete's diet.

3. During the half-time break of a football match the players will drink lots of water. Explain why.

4. Describe how an athlete could increase the amount of carbohydrates stored by their body, before an important event.

1. Exercise will make you more healthy. What does being healthy mean?

2. Give THREE components of 'general fitness'.

i) ....   ii) ....   iii) ....

Suggest how each of these components might be improved by participation in a named sporting activity.

Activity: ....   Activity: ....   Activity: ....

3. Suggest THREE ways in which SOCIAL WELL-BEING could be enhanced by participation in a named activity.

Activity: ....   Activity: ....   Activity: ....

4. Suggest THREE ways in which MENTAL WELL-BEING could be improved as a consequence of participation in a named activity.

Activity: ....   Activity: ....   Activity: ....

1. 'SPECIFICITY' is one 'PRINCIPLE OF TRAINING', what are the other THREE?

   i) ....

   ii) ....

   iii) ....

2. Moving to new and higher levels of fitness can be difficult. Study the graph showing LEVEL OF FITNESS against TIME and answer the following questions.

LEVEL OF FITNESS

PLATEAU

PLATEAU

PLATEAU

TIME

a) When is most progress achieved?

....

b) When is progress more difficult to achieve?

....

c) What is a 'PLATEAU'?

....
....

3. ATROPHY is the deterioration of strength and speed, as muscles lose their tone and size. Can you explain how this condition might be avoided?

....
....
....

4. The body will adapt to the extra demands of training and this must be continuously raised to higher levels if progress is to be made. Can you explain how this might be done, with reference to the following?

   a) Netball ....
   ....
   ....

   b) Football ....
   ....
   ....

   c) Middle distance running ....
   ....

1. **a)** In your own words, describe the difference between 'muscular endurance' and 'muscular strength'.

b) Apart from cycling and running, name THREE sports which require MUSCULAR ENDURANCE.

i)

ii)

iii)

2. **a)** Danny is a weightlifter, his brother Steven is a boxer. For each of them, describe the type of muscular strength they need for their particular sport.

b) Most sports require a combination of the different types of muscular strength. In the table below, fill in the last column with an example of a sport which requires each type in the order of priority shown.

STATIC	EXPLOSIVE	DYNAMIC	EXAMPLE OF SPORT
1	2	3	
3	1	2	
3	2	1	

3. **a)** Which type of muscular strength is most often needed in normal day-to-day living?

b) Which, of muscular strength and muscular endurance, is most needed in normal day-to-day living? Explain your answer.

1. a) Describe how you would improve the type of strength needed for rowing.

b) Describe how you would improve the type of strength needed for being in the front row of a rugby scrum.

c) Describe how you would improve the type of strength needed for the javelin.

TESTING STATIC STRENGTH

TESTING DYNAMIC STRENGTH

25.2

TESTING EXPLOSIVE STRENGTH

2. a) Can you explain why using a 'dynamometer,' which measures hand grip, would be a good way to test static strength.

b) Why do you think doing sit-ups or press-ups would demonstrate someone's dynamic strength?

c) Can you describe a sport in which increased explosive strength would be of use? Explain your answer.

1. a) Give a definition of speed with regard to sports.

    b) i) Apart from football, give TWO examples of sports which require good leg speed.

       ii) Apart from cricket and golf, give TWO examples of sports which require fast arm and torso speed.

    c) Explain why fast arm speed is an advantage in golf.

2. a) State 2 factors which affect the speed of your body's movements.

       i)

       ii)

    b) How can you increase the speed of your body's movements?

    c) If two athletes were to train at the same intensity, under the same conditions, over the same period of time, would they consistently run at the same speed as each other? Explain your answer.

3. Design a training programme which could be carried out over a period of one month to increase the speed of someone of average health. Include how progress could be tested.

1. a) When bones are immobilised for any length of time (e.g. as in a limb fracture), they temporarily lose their mobility. Give TWO reasons for this.

i) ....

ii) ....

b) Give examples of TWO joints which vary greatly in their degree of flexibility.

i) ....

ii) ....

c) Give an example of an injury which may be caused by failure to warm up.

....

2. a) How might a tennis player's warm up routine differ from that of a hurdler?

....

b) Why are gentle stretching exercises a good idea for older people?

....

3. a) How would increased flexibility help a javelin thrower to improve their performance?

....

b) How would increased flexibility help a high jumper to improve their performance?

....

c) How would increased flexibility help a gymnast to improve their performance?

....

1. Fill in the crossword using the clues below.

ACROSS

1. & 7. You should do this properly before starting to exercise (4, 2).
5. Range of movement around a joint (11).
6. A muscle at full stretch (8).
7. (see 1 across)
9. They enable the joints to move (7).
10. You must always do this after exercising (4, 4).
12. It could be walking or playing squash (8).
13. When you are participating in sport you are being this (6).
14. Exercise should be this if you are to benefit fully (7).

DOWN

2. When a muscle is not extended (7).
3. It can assist with a stretch, if care is taken (8, 5).
4. This is done to increase the flexibility of muscles (7).
8. A type of stretching exercise (7).
11. As muscle strength increases, flexibility _____ (9).

When you have completed the crossword, rearrange the letters in the shaded squares to form another word associated with this page.

....

2. Exercises which are designed to increase strength cause muscles to shorten. Why is it important that this type of exercise should be accompanied by stretching exercises?

....
....
....
....

3. Describe TWO methods of testing flexibility.

i) ....
....
ii) ....
....

1. a) For the following sports describe the relative balance needed between aerobic and anaerobic fitness. Express these as a percentage between the two. One has been done for you.

SPORT	ANAEROBIC	AEROBIC	SPORT	ANAEROBIC	AEROBIC
Football	45%	55%	400m Sprint		
Cricket			Sprint Cycling		
Golf			Gymnastics		
Boxing			Diving		
Triathlon			Shot put		

b) What sort of relationship exists between the two types of fitness?

2. a) Describe THREE key characteristics of aerobic training.

b) Describe THREE key characteristics of anaerobic training.

3. a) Describe how aerobic training can be beneficial for people who are involved in endurance events.

b) Describe how anaerobic training can be beneficial for people who are involved in explosive events.

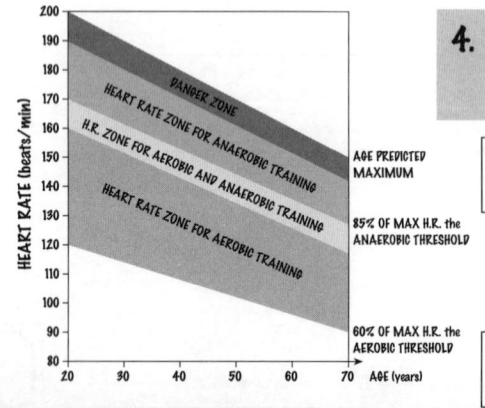

4. a) What would be the maximum recommended heart rate for anaerobic training for someone aged 50?

b) What would be the maximum recommended heart rate for aerobic training for someone aged 30?

1. For the following types of training method, suggest a sport for which each will be beneficial and explain your reasons.

a) Weight training: ....

....

....

b) Interval training: ....

....

....

c) Fartlek training: ....

....

....

d) Circuit training: ....

THREE CIRCUITS

....

....

e) Continuous training: ....

....

....

2. a) Describe the key features of a weight training programme designed to build up strength.

....

....

....

b) Describe the key features of a weight training programme designed to build up endurance.

....

....

....

c) Name TWO sports for which a) and b) would be relevant.

i) .... ii) ....

3. List the benefits of weight training of the human body.

....

....

....

1. What is meant by the term 'circuit training'?

....
....
....

2. Give TWO advantages of circuit training in terms of how muscle groups are worked.

i) ....
....

ii) ....
....

3. a) Circuits can be designed to improve various aspects of fitness and personal performance.
    In the space provided design a circuit for a named activity or personal target.

    b) How could you measure if progress was being made, and if so, how could the circuit be modified to
    ensure further progress?

....
....
....
....

4. Circuit training can improve MUSCLE TONE. List SIX other beneficial effects.

i) .... ii) .... iii) ....

iv) .... v) .... vi) ....

1. 'Interval Training' and 'Fartlek Training' are quite similar and therefore have similar effects on the body.

   a) What are the THREE main benefits?

   i) ....

   ii) ....

   iii) ....

   b) Briefly describe the similarities and differences.

   Interval Training: ....

   ....

   ....

   Fartlek Training: ....

   ....

   ....

   c) Apart from running, cycling and swimming, which sports and activities are these types of training most suited to?

   ....

   ....

   ....

2. **a) Briefly describe what CONTINUOUS TRAINING involves.**

   ....

   ....

   ....

   b) What are its effects on the body and who might gain most benefit from this type of training?

   ....

   ....

   ....

3. Assuming that a performer's basic fitness levels are good enough,
   how might PRESSURE TRAINING be more advantageous than other types of training?

   ....

   ....

   ....

1. The closed season for many sports, particularly football, has become shorter and shorter, to the extent that the football closed season is now little more than a month. Explain the reasons why this has taken place and list the dangers that this development may result in.

2. Describe how 12 months in the life of an athlete may be broken up.

3. Describe how 12 months in the life of a rugby player may be broken up.

1. Name THREE muscles vital to the circulatory and respiratory systems.

i) ....

ii) ....

iii) ....

2. What happens to these muscles when they are subjected to long term training?

3. What effect does this have on the circulatory or respiratory system?

4. Why do many top ENDURANCE ATHLETES train at altitude before major competitions? Try to explain your answers fully and indicate the advantage of any training adaptations which you suggest might occur.

5. How does LONG TERM TRAINING improve the body's ability to make use of oxygen?

6. Which effects of LONG TERM TRAINING make an athlete less likely to become injured?

1. Complete the following paragraph using the words below.

| harder | exercise | lactic acid | glucose | energy | aerobically | increases |

| intense | carbon dioxide | anaerobically | oxygen | heart | increases | lungs | oxygen |

When we start to .... our muscles need to work .... In order to do this, they need to transfer more .... Muscles prefer transferring energy .... because it is more efficient than transferring energy .... The .... and .... try to get as much .... to the working muscles as possible. The heart rate .... and respiratory rate also .... This enables more .... and .... to be taken to the working muscles and more .... to be taken away. If the activity is very .... the body will transfer energy and produce ....

2. What does the term 'vasodilation' mean?

3. What are the TWO effects of vasodilation?

i)

ii)

4. Describe THREE short term responses to a named and mostly aerobic activity of your choice.

AEROBIC ACTIVITY:

i)

ii)

iii)

5. Describe THREE short term responses to a named and mostly anaerobic activity of your choice.

ANAEROBIC ACTIVITY:

i)

ii)

iii)

1. What part of the body controls the core temperature?

2. a) During intense exercise what adaptations might occur in the body?

b) What adaptations might occur in the body on a cold day?

c) Explain the differences in the appearance of the skin which would occur in a) and b).

3. a) List THREE ways in which the body can become dehydrated.

i)

ii)

iii)

b) Explain the changes which occur within the body when the blood water level becomes too low.

c) Explain what would happen if you drank 3 pints of water within 15 minutes.

1. a) Describe what is involved in the multi-stage fitness test.

b) What does this test set out to measure?

2. a) Describe what is involved in the Cooper Test.

b) What is this test designed to measure?

3. a) Describe what is involved in the Harvard Step Test.

b) What calculation must be used?

c) What is it designed to measure?

4. a) Describe what is involved in the Cycle Ergonometer Test.

b) What measurements must be taken?

1. a) Describe, in your own words, how you could test someone's agility.

b) Explain why this is a good way to test agility.

2. a) Explain why balance and coordination are important when training or exercising.

b) How could you improve your coordination?

c) If you tested your coordination and then practised to improve it, what results would you expect to see the next time you tested it and how would this be shown?

3. a) Why is reaction time important in sport?

b) List 3 instances in sport in which a quick reaction time is particularly important.

i)

ii)

iii)

4. a) A class of students want to test their individual explosive strength. Why is it important for each of them to make 2 chalk marks if they use the 'Sergeant Jump'?

b) List 2 sports in which explosive strength is required and explain why it is needed.

i)

ii)

1. Describe the THREE phases involved in a thorough warm up.

i) ....

....

....

ii) ....

....

....

iii) ....

....

....

....

2. Suggest THREE problems which could occur if any of these phases was neglected.

i) ....

ii) ....

iii) ....

3. a) Explain the physiological reasons why athletes continue to jog around the track at the end of their race.

....

....

....

....

b) Describe THREE problems which may occur if athletes don't warm down properly.

i) ....

....

ii) ....

....

iii) ....

....

1. Label the diagram below, to highlight the features of a sports shoe which makes it appropriate for a named sporting activity. You can make amendments to the diagram.

Sporting Activity: ....

2. Give TWO reasons why many sports people have spikes or studs on their shoes or boots.

i) ....
....
ii) ....
....

3. Why would it not be appropriate for a rugby or football player to use spikes?

....
....
....

4. Describe TWO other kinds of specialist footwear and explain their features.

i) ....
....
....
ii) ....
....
....

1. Suggest a safety aspect that players should consider before and during a named activity.

i) Before Activity:

ii) After Activity:

2. Suggest TWO possible outcomes of neglecting these safety considerations.

i)

ii)

3. PE teachers should insist that pupils remove any jewellery before the start of a PE lesson. State whether you agree or disagree with this statement and justify your answer.

4. a) Name TWO games/activities and describe TWO safety checks which an official should make before the start of each.

i) Game/Activity:

Safety Checks:

ii) Game/Activity:

Safety Checks:

b) Suggest the possible consequences of these checks being neglected.

i)

ii)

1. Complete the following crossword.

DOWN

1. Prevents the body from sweating. (14)
2. Can cause blisters, bunions and corns. (5, 5)
3. Contagious warts on the foot. (8)
4. Could be caused by ill-fitting or new shoes. (8)
6. Helps to hide the smell of sweat. (9)
7. Can restrict vision. (4, 4)
12. Calluses of thick skin. (5)
13 & 15. It is important to keep .... to prevent bacteria from breeding. (7, 5)

ACROSS

1. A fungal growth between the toes caused by not drying feet properly. (8, 4)
5. A piece of protective equipment used for teeth. (3, 6)
8. Shin pads offer the shins some ..... from bad challenges. (10)
9. Inflammation of the joint capsule caused by tight shoes. (7)
10. Protected by a gum shield. (5)
11. Can prevent other people becoming infected with a verruca. (4)
14. Injury to another player, if your nails are too long. (10)
16. Could be used to treat or prevent athletes foot. (6, 6)

2. Describe the cause, symptoms and treatment of a named foot infection.

Infection: ....
....

3. Describe the symptoms of a common foot problem, caused as a result of ill-fitting shoes.

1. Study the diagrams below and answer the questions.

A   B   C   D   E   F   G   H

a) Which of the diagrams display GOOD POSTURE. Give reasons for your answers.

i)

ii)

iii)

iv)

b) What is meant by POOR POSTURE?

c) Tiredness, poor nutrition and inappropriate clothing can contribute to the causes of poor posture. Give FOUR other possible causes.

i)   ii)

iii)   iv)

2. How can regular exercise improve posture?

3. List THREE POSTURAL DEFECTS and the problems they could cause.

i)

ii)

iii)

1. What is the objective of FIRST AID treatment?

2. Who is qualified to carry out FIRST AID procedures?

3. What do the letters D, R and A B C refer to in terms of FIRST AID?

D: ....   R: ....

A: ....   B: ....   C: ....

4. Briefly summarise stages A, B and C of the DR ABC procedure using the illustrations to guide you.

a)

b)

c)

5. What is the purpose of putting the casualty in the RECOVERY POSITION? Give FOUR reasons.

i) ....   ii) ....

iii) ....   iv) ....

6. What other vital measure must a FIRST AIDER take?

1. a) Having completed the ABC procedure, under what circumstances might MOUTH TO MOUTH RESUSCITATION (rescue breathing) be required?

b) What is the objective of MOUTH TO MOUTH RESUSCITATION?

2. Describe the THREE stages of MOUTH TO MOUTH RESUSCITATION illustrated below.

a)

b)

c)

3. How many breaths would you give in one minute to ...

i) ... an adult: ii) ... a child:

4. a) If the casualty STARTS TO BREATHE ON THEIR OWN and STILL HAS A PULSE what should you do?

b) If the casualty DOES NOT START TO BREATHE ON THEIR OWN and STILL HAS A PULSE what should you do?

c) If the casualty DOES NOT START TO BREATHE ON THEIR OWN and NOW HAS NO PULSE what should you do?

1. How would you recognise that CARDIAC MASSAGE should be carried out on a casualty?

2. What is the objective of CARDIAC MASSAGE?

3. When carrying out CARDIAC MASSAGE ...

   a) ... how do you locate the massage point?

   b) ... which part of the hand should be applied?

   c) How deep should the compression be for ...

    i) ... an adult: .... cm   ii) ... a child: .... cm

   d) What is the rate at which compressions should be made?

4. CARDIAC MASSAGE must be alternated with MOUTH TO MOUTH RESUSCITATION.

   a) Explain why:

   b) What is the ratio of breaths to compressions?

5. Complete the following statements:

   a) If the casualty STARTS TO BREATHE and HAS A PULSE, you should ...

   b) If the casualty DOES NOT START TO BREATHE and HAS A PULSE, you should ...

   c) If the casualty DOES NOT START TO BREATHE and HAS NO PULSE, you should ...

1. What do the letters R.I.C.E. refer to in terms of First Aid?

R .... | I .... | C .... | E ....

2. Explain the purpose of each component of the R.I.C.E. Treatment.

R ....

I ....

C ....

E ....

3. In a named sporting activity ...

a) ... describe a situation which could result in a STRAIN, how you would identify it, and how you would treat it.

STRAIN: Activity ....

b) ... describe a situation which could result in a SPRAIN, how you would identify it, and how you would treat it.

SPRAIN: Activity ....

4. What is a BRUISE, how might one occur, and how would you treat one?

....

1. **a)** What symptoms would make you suspect someone had CONCUSSION?

b) Describe a situation, in a sporting activity, when concussion might occur.

c) What measures would you take if the casualty became unconscious?

2. **a)** What is a FRACTURE and how might it occur in a sporting activity?

b) Describe the symptoms and the measures you would take.

Symptoms:

Measures:

3. DISLOCATION is the dislodging of a bone or bones at a joint.

a) In what type of sporting circumstances might this occur?

b) How would you identify it?

c) What should you do?

4. **a)** How might a knee cartilage be injured?

b) What signs would you look for?

1. a) Unscramble the following words. They are all injuries or ailments.

i) ATHEDDYNIOR	v) CHOKS
ii) GRASSACUDENZT	vi) PARCM
iii) HEPOMYATHRI	vii) ATTREESHOK
iv) THENAXATHESIUO	viii) THICTS

b) Use the words from part a) and describe the main characteristics associated with them.

i) .... : ....

ii) .... : ....

iii) .... : ....

iv) .... : ....

v) .... : ....

vi) .... : ....

vii) .... : ....

viii) .... : ....

1. a) Complete this crossword about factors which can affect performance.

ACROSS

3. Tightness. (7)

5. Athletes may train at .... (8)

7. These help you get better or banned! (5)

9. To do with the body. (13)

16. This can affect air and water. (9)

17. Stress. (7)

18. Sun, rain or wind. (7)

19. Reactions inside of you? (4, 9)

DOWN

1. Fracture, sprain, strain. (6)

2. It affects everyone. (3)

4. Tiredness. (7)

6. Sometimes this can hold people back. (10)

8. Unwell. (3)

10. Talent, artistry. (5)

11. A large one could make you nervous or spur you on! (5)

12. Introvert, extrovert. (11)

13. Blood .... increases oxygen supply. (6)

14. You need this to get going. (10)

15. Term used to differentiate between males and females. (6)

b) Highlight the ENVIRONMENTAL, PSYCHOLOGICAL and PHYSIOLOGICAL factors in different colours. Can you think of any others?

i) Environmental: ....

ii) Psychological: ....

iii) Physiological: ....

1. List 4 environmental factors which could affect a sportsperson's performance.

i) ....   iii) ....

ii) ....   iv) ....

2. a) Which environmental factor might enhance the performance of anaerobic events?

....

b) Which environmental factor might reduce performance in endurance events?

....

c) Why do you think humidity would affect temperature regulation?

....

d) Why would short passing tactics be beneficial in windy conditions?

....

3. a) Do you think you would experience more pressure and stress when playing a sport as part of a team or as an individual? Explain your answer.

....

....

....

b) Explain as fully as you can why playing in front of a crowd might increase the pressure a sportsperson feels.

....

....

c) Why would stress have a negative effect on performance?

....

d) Explain how stress could have a positive effect on performance.

....

....

4. Why should an athlete always ensure that they have had a good night's sleep before a major event?

....

....

1. For the following somatotype charts, describe the characteristics of the person represented by the chart and the sort of sports he/she may be best suited to.

a)

b)

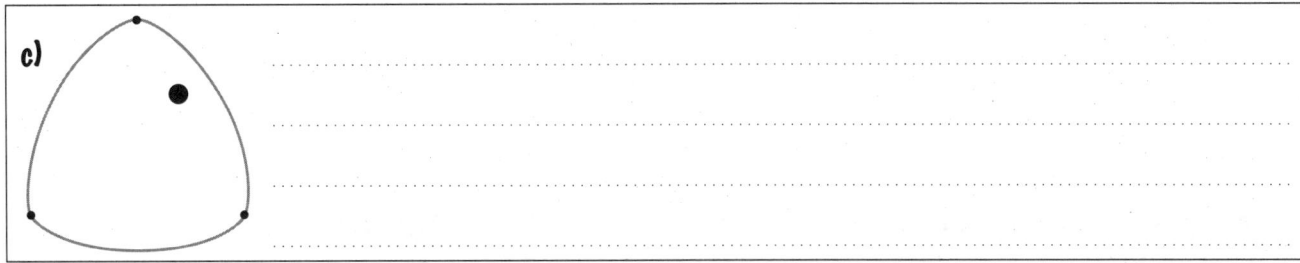

c)

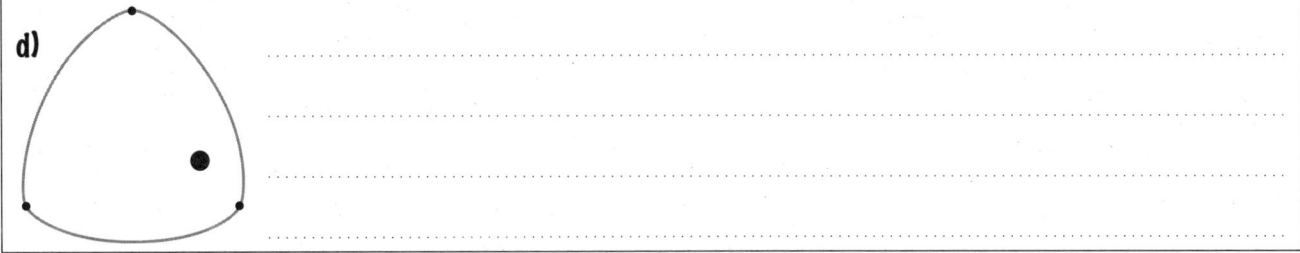

d)

2. Describe the physical characteristics of:

a) An extreme mesomorph:

b) An extreme ectomorph:

c) An extreme endomorph:

3. On the chart opposite, mark the likely position of the following sports people:

a) Gymnast

b) Wrestler

c) Sprinter

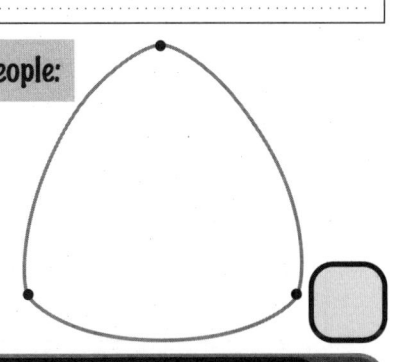

1. The men's world records in athletic events are faster, further and higher than those set by women. Explain why these differences exist in the world record standards for the following events.

   a) 100m Men's world record   9.78 sec   Tim Montgomery 2002

       100m Women's world record   10.49 sec   Florence Griffith-Joyner 1988

   ....
   ....
   ....
   ....

   b) Marathon Men's world record   2'04.55   Paul Tergat 2003

       Marathon Women's world record   2'15.25   Paula Radcliffe 2003

   ....
   ....
   ....
   ....

   c) Javelin Men's world record   98.48m   Jan Zelezny 1996

       Javelin Women's world record   71.54m   Osleidys Menendez 2001

   ....
   ....
   ....
   ....

2. Explain why most athletics world records are set by athletes below the age of 35.

   ....
   ....
   ....
   ....

3. Identify FIVE characteristics of a) a healthy lifestyle and b) an unhealthy lifestyle.

   a) i) ....   b) i) ....

      ii) ....   ii) ....

      iii) ....   iii) ....

      iv) ....   iv) ....

      v) ....   v) ....

1. Describe the characteristics of a named sportsperson who you think has an extrovert personality.

Name:

Characteristics:

2. Describe the characteristics of a named sportsperson who you think has an introvert personality.

Name:

Characteristics:

3. a) Describe a sporting situation in which a performer could suffer from anxiety or tension.

b) Describe how a person might recognise themselves as suffering from anxiety or tension.

4. a) Describe a situation in which you can recall being 'well motivated.' Identify what motivated you.

b) Describe a situation in which you can recall having a lot of ADRENALINE.
Describe how your body felt at the time.

5. a) Define DIRECT AGGRESSION.

b) Define INDIRECT AGGRESSION.

1. a) Name THREE drugs which athletes could use to improve their performance.

> i) .... ii) .... iii) ....

b) Explain how these drugs could improve performance.

> i) ....
>
> ....
>
> ii) ....
>
> ....
>
> iii) ....
>
> ....

c) Identify the negative effects that these drugs can have on the body.

> i) ....
>
> ....
>
> ii) ....
>
> ....
>
> iii) ....
>
> ....

2. a) What kind of drug might be used to help a boxer lose weight before a bout?

> ....

b) Why can this be dangerous?

> ....

3. Why do some sportsmen and sportswomen rely on alcohol and tobacco when they have no performance enhancing effect?

> ....
>
> ....

4. Explain fully what is meant by BLOOD DOPING.

> ....
>
> ....

1. a) Name a sportsperson you believe to be skilful.

....

b) Justify why you have chosen this person. Refer to the definition of skill in your answer.

....

2. Categorise the following skills as being predominantly open or closed.

Making a tackle in a rugby game

Shot put

Skiing

Passing a football in a match

A tennis game

Serving in tennis

b) Describe as fully as you can the differences between 'whole' and 'part' practice.

....

3. There are FOUR ways in which you can practice. Suggest which type of practice would best suit the following.

Badminton Smash

Bowling in Cricket

Tackling in Hockey

Shooting in Netball

4. Using a variety of techniques is often the best way of helping someone learn a new skill. Describe the methods you would use to teach someone how to throw the discus.

....

1. Feedback is vital for improved performance. Discuss this statement.

2. a) There are TWO components of feedback. Name them.

   i)

   ii)

   b) Give an example of each component of feedback in a named sporting activity.

   i)

   ii)

   KP + KR

3. Which of these two components of feedback are, in your opinion, of most value. Use sporting examples to justify your answer.

4. If a coach told you that you didn't play well last week, he/she would not be providing you with effective feedback. Why?

1. a) State one effect that technology has had in golf.

b) How has technology affected football? Mention at least two examples.

c) Explain how a 200m sprint can be made fairer using ICT.

2. Imagine you were coaching a top tennis player. What technological developments might you make use of and why?

3. a) How might a heart rate monitor benefit an athlete?

b) Explain whether heart rate monitors are only beneficial for top athletes.

4. a) Why would it be beneficial to have power analysis sensors in running shoes?

b) What other sport(s) might benefit from power analysis sensors and why?

1. a) If a sports club wants to attract commercial sponsorship, what must it be able to offer to the potential sponsors?

b) Give THREE examples of the type of exposure a sponsor of a premiership football club might expect.

i)

ii)

iii)

c) Give FOUR examples of the way money from sponsorship might be used.

i) ii)

iii) iv)

2. a) Apart from a lack of spectator interest, what other factor (or factors) might dissuade sponsors from investing in a particular sport?

b) Give TWO actual examples of sponsorship in sport.

i) ii)

3. Describe how sponsorship has influenced the following ...

a) ... the aftermatch interviews following a premiership football match.

b) ... the physical appearance of racing cars and the outfits worn by drivers.

c) ... the schedule for the 1994 Football World Cup in the USA.

d) ... the timing of the Rugby League season.

1. a) Why do sports like hockey, netball and badminton attract fewer sponsors than football and rugby?

    b) If you were looking to sponsor some aspect of sport, which are the THREE most important factors you would consider?

    i)

    ii)

    iii)

2. Some sports will not accept sponsorship from certain types of business. Name ONE of these businesses and give reasons why it is not acceptable.

3. a) Describe THREE advantages and THREE disadvantages of sponsorship to a sport or a performer.

ADVANTAGES	DISADVANTAGES	£
i)	i)	
ii)	ii)	
iii)	iii)	

    b) Describe THREE advantages of sponsorship to a business or individual sponsor.

    i)

    ii)

    iii)

    c) Suggest THREE reasons why a business or individual might withdraw their sponsorship.

    i)

    ii)

    iii)

4. What advantage do sports like Rugby League and Rugby Union have over Football when it comes to attracting certain types of sponsor? Explain your answer fully.

1. The media delivers information in different forms. Describe FOUR of these media forms and the type of coverage they are able to provide.

i) ....

....

ii) ....

....

iii) ....

....

iv) ....

....

2. Media coverage can affect how the public forms its opinions on sport and sporting personalities through its presentation of pictures and articles. Describe:

a) ONE harmful or negative effect and give TWO examples.

Effect: ....

Example 1: ....

Example 2: ....

b) ONE beneficial or positive effect and give TWO examples.

Effect: ....

Example 1: ....

Example 2: ....

3. Participation in sport can be promoted by the various forms of media. Using THREE examples, explain how the media can improve the image of, and participation in, a named activity.

i) ....

....

....

ii) ....

....

....

iii) ....

....

1. Live media coverage can affect attendances at sporting events. Explain TWO positive and TWO negative effects using examples.

POSITIVE:

i)

ii)

NEGATIVE:

i)

ii)

2. Using examples in TWO named activities, explain how the media has influenced rule changes, and why.

i)

ii)

3. Explain the link between the MEDIA, SPONSORSHIP and SPORT, in terms of the finance generated.

1. What are the advantages for the players and performers of spectators attending sporting events?

2. Explain what is meant by sporting 'etiquette' and give TWO examples from different sports.

3. 'Contact sports result in violent behaviour while non-contact sports result in non-violent behaviour among spectators'. Give TWO arguments <u>for</u> this statement and TWO arguments <u>against</u> it.

FOR:

i)

ii)

AGAINST:

i)

ii)

4. Spectators may also behave badly at events due to the actions of officials. Explain why this may be so using examples.

5. Describe measures which have been taken (or might be taken) to ensure good crowd behaviour at sporting events.

1. What are the TWO main differences between 'amateur' and 'professional' sports people?

AMATEURS:

i) ....

ii) ....

PROFESSIONALS:

i) ....

ii) ....

2. Who decides whether a competitor is amateur, professional or semi-professional and how?

....

3. Many 'amateurs' retain their status but do their sport full-time. Give THREE ways in which this can happen, with a brief explanation.

i) ....

ii) ....

iii) ....

4. Explain, using specific examples, what is meant by an 'open' event in sport.

....

5. Find TWELVE words associated with AMATEUR/PROFESSIONAL sport and list them.

```
X  J  M  W  H  A  B  L  E  M  U
M  D  O  N  R  G  R  A  N  T  S
B  L  N  B  Y  E  E  T  O  N  S
U  V  E  Z  E  N  W  E  S  K  U
C  M  Y  F  M  T  B  A  T  A  T
A  B  O  R  U  L  E  S  R  R  A
N  C  A  R  E  E  R  C  U  D  T
S  I  T  T  L  M  U  L  S  M  S
W  H  A  K  E  E  A  R  T  U  J
E  E  N  A  T  N  I  R  F  L  A
Z  O  E  E  E  K  F  E  U  E  N
R  E  Y  P  A  Y  M  E  N  T  G
G  D  O  G  N  O  M  E  D  O  W
```

1. ....
2. ....
3. ....
4. ....
5. ....
6. ....
7. ....
8. ....
9. ....
10. ....
11. ....
12. ....

1. Sports facilities are often purpose built to serve the local community.
   Give ONE example of a single-activity and a 'multi-activity' facility, and who might use them.

   i) Single-Activity: ....
   ....
   ii) Multi-Activity: ....
   ....

2. Some specialist sports facilities take advantage of the natural environment. Describe TWO sports which require natural features.

   i) ....
   ....
   ii) ....
   ....

3. Explain THREE ways in which local sports facilities can be provided.

   i) ....
   ....
   ii) ....
   ....
   iii) ....
   ....

4. Hotel groups which operate nationwide often have sports/leisure facilities to cater for guests and private members. Describe TWO other 'national' organisations which provide facilities 'nationally' and the people who might use them.

   i) ....
   ii) ....

5. The 'location' of sports facilities depends on a number of factors. Planning permission and Costs are two of them. List THREE others and explain why they are important.

   i) ....
   ii) ....
   iii) ....

1. In order to function efficiently a sports club requires 'appointed officials.' Fill in the blanks and write a brief description of each official's duties.

i) M _ _ _ S _ _ P _ S _ C _ _ _ _

....

ii) C _ B _ _ _ R _ A _ _ _ _

....

....

iii) _ X _ U _ S _ S _ _ _ T _ Y

....

....

iv) H _ _ P _ S _

....

....

v) _ R _ S _ _ R _ _

....

....

vi) These elected members will form a .... M _ T _ _ E to organise and run the facilities, competitions, coaching and development.

2. State and describe THREE ways a club would raise income to fund its activities.

i) ....

ii) ....

iii) ....

3. How and why do clubs develop links with schools and the local communities?

....
....
....
....
....

1. Sport at all levels, from local clubs to the National Teams, requires large amounts of money to operate. Some is spent on developing SPORTS FACILITIES and EVERYDAY RUNNING COSTS.
List THREE other factors which require financing and give a brief explanation of each.

i) ....

....

ii) ....

....

iii) ....

....

2. A sports club gains financial income from a number of sources. Fill in the blanks and give a brief explanation of each.

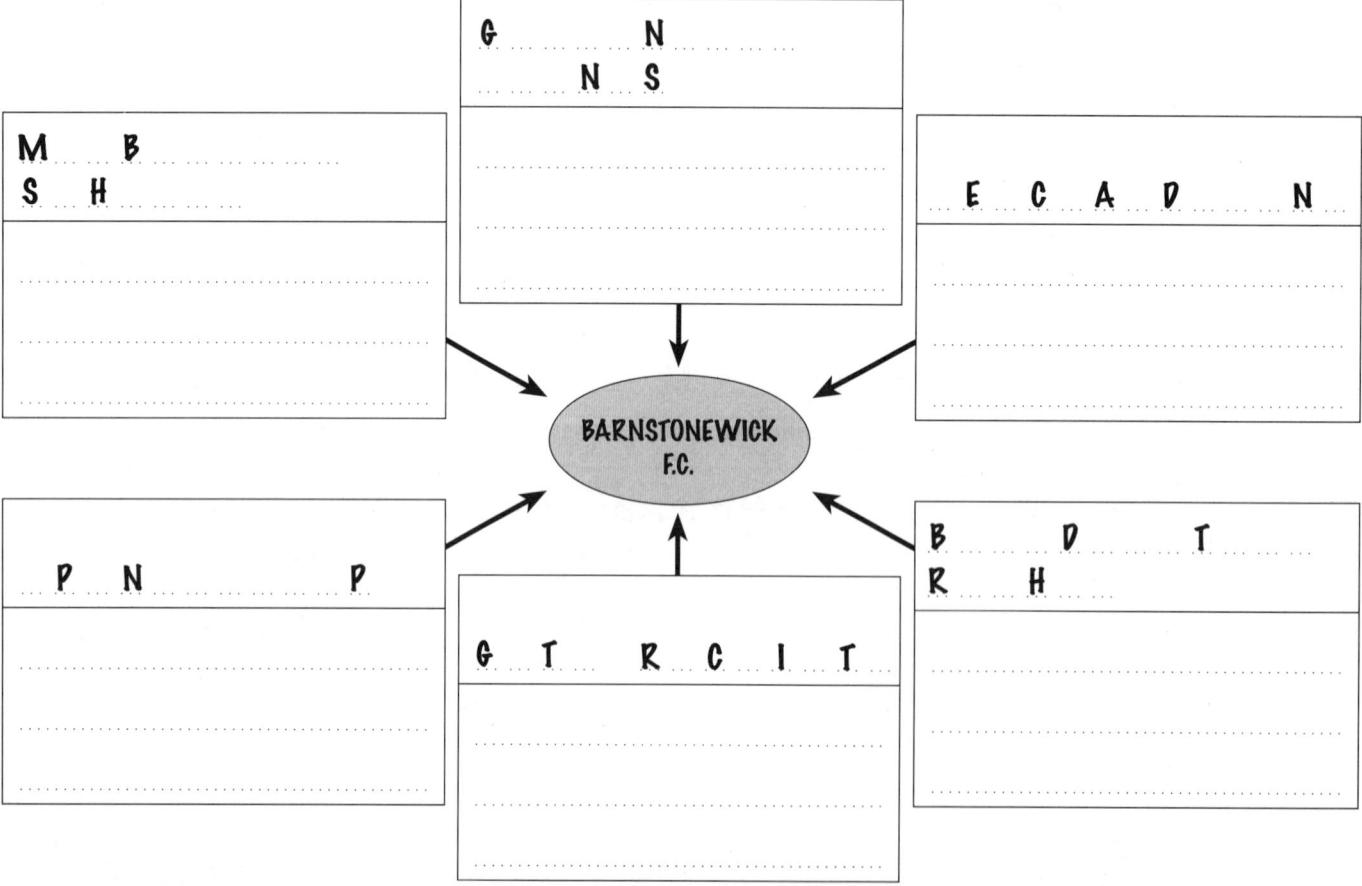

G ___ N ___
N ___ S ___

M ___ B ___
S ___ H ___

E ___ C ___ A ___ D ___ N ___

BARNSTONEWICK F.C.

P ___ N ___ P ___

G ___ T ___ R ___ C ___ I ___ T ___

B ___ D ___ T ___
R ___ H ___

3. In recent years football, rugby league and rugby union have received large sums of money in return for 'broadcasting rights.' Briefly explain how some of this money has been spent by the clubs.

....

....

....

....

Use pg 69 in your revision guide to find out the answers to the following questions ...

1. a) Which Olympic Games have been boycotted by countries protesting over various issues?

....

b) Which Olympic Games saw black athletes giving the 'Black Power' salute to draw attention to civil rights' problems in the USA?

....

c) Which Olympic Games resulted in a huge financial burden for the city which hosted the summer games?

....

d) In which Olympic Games were athletes taken hostage because of political issues?

....

e) In which Olympic Games did Hitler refuse to acknowledge the success of the black United States athlete Jesse Owens?

....

f) In which Olympic Games was there a boycott by the USSR as a possible retaliation against America for a previous Olympics?

....

g) Which Olympics saw the re-admittance of the South African team and for the first time, since before the Second World War, a unified German team?

....

h) In which Olympics was the man who broke the 100m record in the final stripped of his gold medal after testing positive for drugs?

....

1. a) Who actually arranges international sporting events?

....

b) Who actually decides where the events are held?

....

c) Why are so many countries keen to stage major international events?

....
....
....
....

d) What risks do these countries take when they decide to apply to host an international event?

....
....
....
....

2. a) How can ordinary people living in a host nation benefit from a major international event?

....
....
....
....

b) How do sportsmen and sportswomen within the host nation benefit from the staging of major international events?

....
....
....
....

3. List FIVE major qualities which a potential host to a major event should provide. List these in order of priority.

i. ....
ii. ....
iii. ....
iv. ....
v. ....

1. Describe FOUR reasons why National Governments try to encourage sporting excellence.

i) ....

....

ii) ....

....

iii) ....

....

iv) ....

....

2. Countries around the world promote sport in different ways and they try to develop approaches which bring success.

a) Describe the U.K.'s approach to sport in terms of encouraging MASS PARTICIPATION and developing ELITE TALENT.

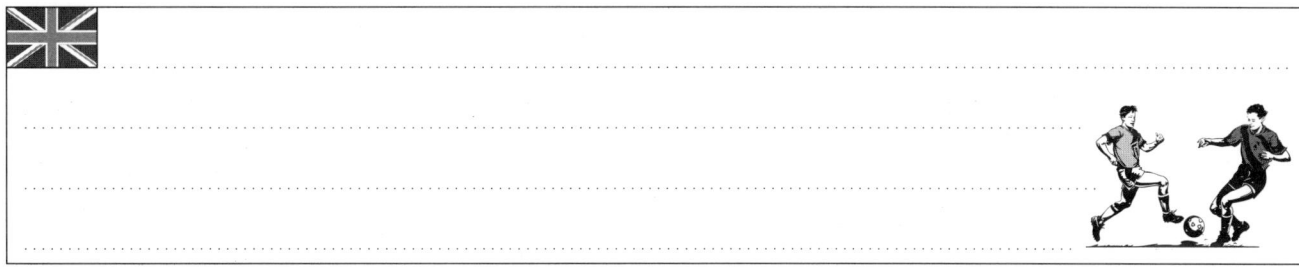

b) Describe the U.S.A.'s school and college system to develop top performers and create public interest.

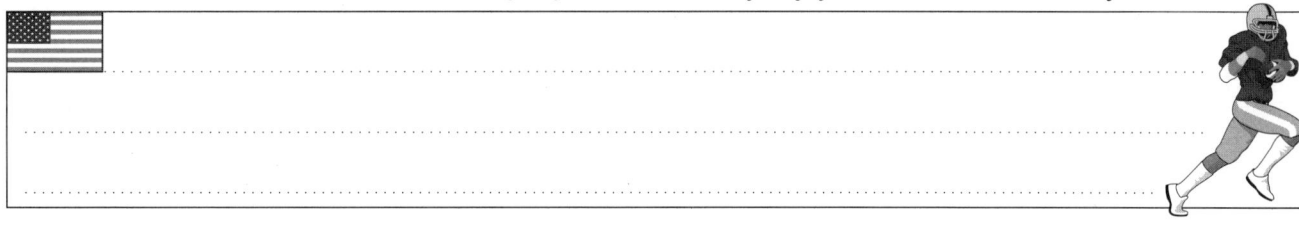

c) Explain how former Eastern Bloc countries managed to produce world class 'amateur' sports people prior to the break-up of the communist system in 1989.

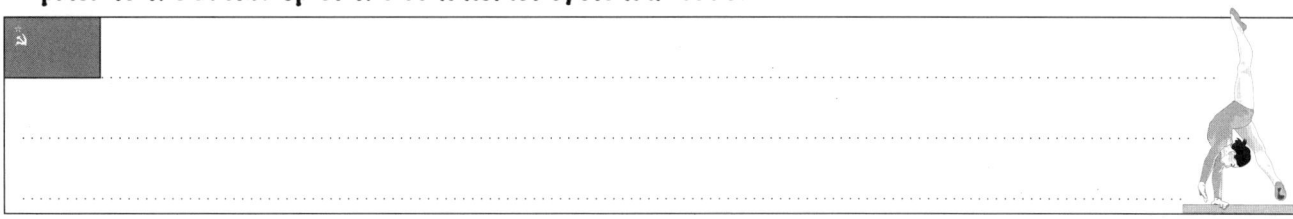

d) Explain why Third World developing nations tend to produce good athletes and footballers.

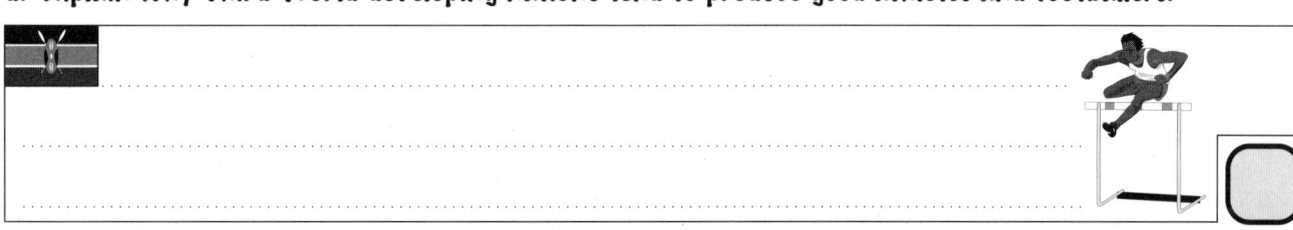

1. Schools have an important role in promoting and providing opportunities to take part in sport. Describe THREE ways in which this occurs.

i) ....

....

ii) ....

....

iii) ....

2. Explain briefly why schools provide Physical Education.

....

....

3. Physical Education has strong links with 'health education' which is promoted in other lessons. In which subjects might the following topics be taught?

TOPIC	LESSON	WHY?
Diet		
Personal Hygiene		
Health and Fitness		
Drugs Awareness		
Social Relationships		

4. The activities available to pupils depend on a number of factors. List and briefly describe FOUR of these factors.

i) ....

ii) ....

iii) ....

iv) ....

1. Complete this crossword using the clues below.

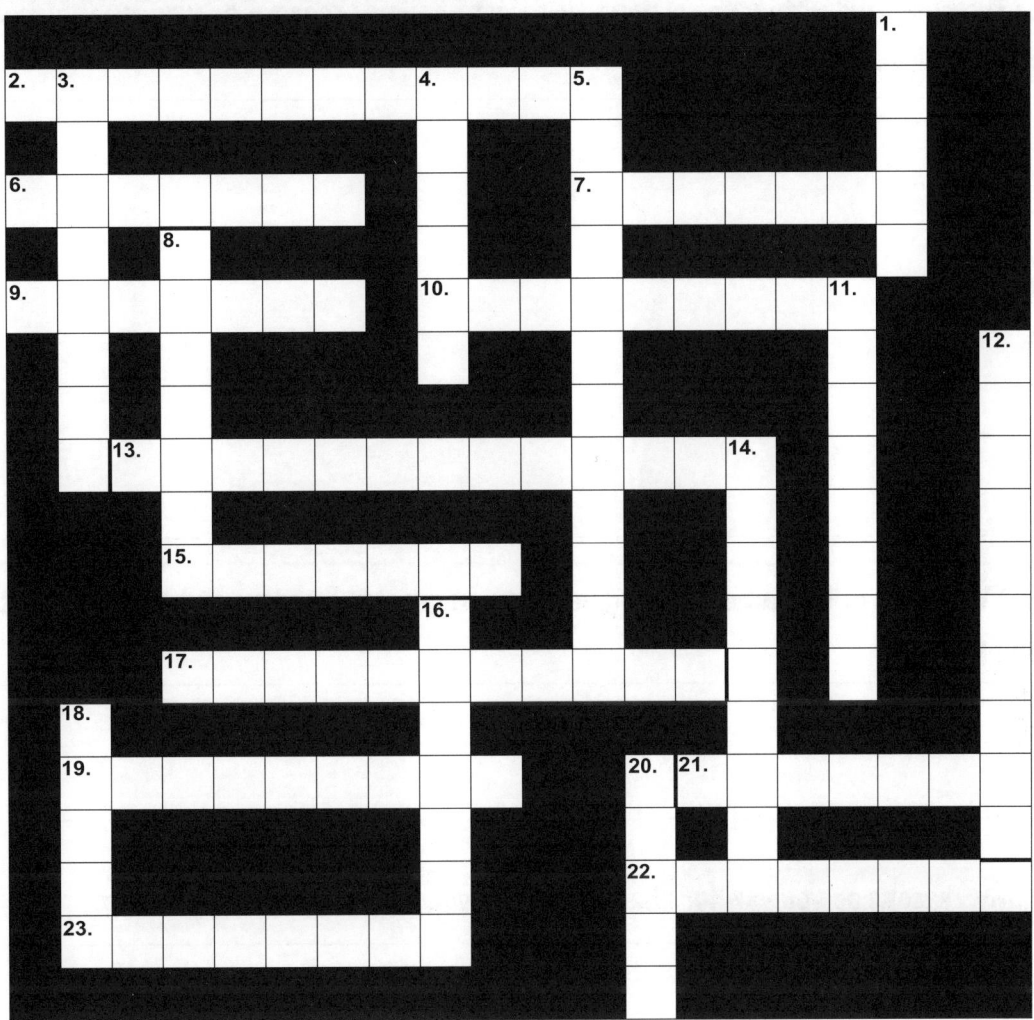

ACROSS

2. Those privileged few who enjoyed sport in the 19th Century. (12)
6. A bicycle is needed for this. (7)
7. Lawn sport involving hoops and mallets. (7)
9. Restricted. (7)
10. In the 19th Century sport was mainly .... (9)
13. An old fashioned bicycle with a large front wheel. (5, 8)
15. Sport can be a reflection of this. (7)
17. The improvement of things such as technology. (11)
19. Only available to a few. (9)
21. Not a professional. (7)
22. Recognition of the b .... of physical recreation. (8)
23. Professional sports people do lots of t .... to achieve their best. (8)

DOWN

1. Top-class, selected few. (5)
3. Sport or .... recreation. (8)
4. Its where you study and sometimes play sport. (6)
5. It reflects a change in attitudes. (12)
8. Different people have different levels. (7)
11. When not fully abled. (8)
12. Social change resulted in better h .... (10)
14. Men of higher social standing. (9)
16. Slow, running motion. (7)
18. An organised competitive activity. (5)
20. A pastime which is regularly enjoyed. (5)

1. a) The traditional view, in the early part of this century and before that, was that a woman's place was in the home and not on the playing field. List as many reasons as you can which were used to support this view.

b) Which TWO Acts of Parliament have given women greater freedom and therefore raised their sporting profile?

i)

ii)

2. List as many reasons as you can for the increased involvement of women in sport.

3. Although there is still much more to be done, there is much greater provision for the disabled athlete nowadays. Much of this was due to Disability Sport England (1994). List the improvements this made for disabled athletes.

1. Because of the benefits of Physical Recreation, the government has a policy to encourage greater public participation.

   a) How can LOCAL AUTHORITIES encourage participation in sporting activities (including minority groups)?

   b) Which other organisations can offer support to LOCAL AUTHORITIES?

   i) .... ii) ....

2. One of the roles of the HOME COUNTRY SPORTS COUNCILS is to get more people of all ages and abilities involved in physical activity. Describe TWO promotional campaigns and the reasons for them.

   i) ....

   ii) ....

3. Participation in some activities has grown whilst in some others it has declined. Choose ONE example of each and give reasons for their growth or decline.

   Growth Activity: ....

   Activity in decline: ....

4. How would you encourage people to get involved in sport?

1. Describe THREE reasons why people participate in, or become involved in sport or physical recreation.

i) ....

ii) ....

iii) ....

2. Describe SIX ways in which a person can become involved in sport or physical recreation.
Link your six examples to the appropriate reasons given in your answer to question 1, and state what qualifications and qualities are needed.

i) ....

....

ii) ....

....

iii) ....

....

iv) ....

....

v) ....

....

vi) ....

....

3. The leisure industry is a growth area which provides opportunities for people to become involved in sport and physical recreation. Name FOUR such opportunities.

i) ....

ii) ....

iii) ....

iv) ....

4. Name FOUR other types of sport-related careers and give a brief explanation of what they involve.

i) ....

ii) ....

iii) ....

iv) ....

1. a) Social Groups can have an important influence on a person's participation in sport. The 'Peer Group' is one of these. Name FOUR others.

b) Using PEER PRESSURE as an example, describe FOUR negative and FOUR positive effects it can have on a person taking part in physical activity.

GROUP PRESSURE	
NEGATIVE	**POSITIVE**
i)	i)
ii)	ii)
iii)	iii)
iv)	iv)

2. List SIX factors which might affect a person's participation in physical activity. Try to make two significant points for each factor.

a) .... i) ....
   ii) ....

b) .... i) ....
   ii) ....

c) .... i) ....
   ii) ....

d) .... i) ....
   ii) ....

e) .... i) ....
   ii) ....

f) .... i) ....
   ii) ....

1. a) Explain, in your own words, how a ladder system is used in sports competitions.

....

    b) What are the advantages and disadvantages of using this type of system?

....

2. a) What advantages does the league system have over the ladder system?

....

    b) Why would it be a good idea to score as many goals as possible in every game if your team was in a league table?

....

3. a) Explain fully how a knock out system works.

....

    b) Describe the system which is employed to try to ensure that the best players don't knock each other out too early in a competition.

....

    c) State the advantages of this system.

....

4. Which of the three methods do you think results in the most interesting sporting event for spectators? Explain your answer.

....

1. a) What is leisure time?

....

b) Explain some of the reasons why some people may now have more leisure time available, with reference to the HOME and WORK.

Home: ....

....

Work: ....

....

2. An increase in leisure time has led to a growth in the 'leisure industry' which provides leisure facilities. Name the THREE categories of leisure facility providers and give some examples of the type of facilities they operate.

i) ....

ii) ....

iii) ....

3. How does the leisure industry provide for people with more time but less money e.g. OAP's, unemployed?

....

1. A young child playing at a sporting activity in a park or local playing field with family and friends shows a particular talent and enjoyment of the activity.

   a) Where could the child go to develop this talent and who could help develop it?

   b) If the child continues to develop his/her talent what would be the usual progression from 'grass roots' to 'elite performer'?

   c) How would the level of coaching change, as the child begins to fulfil his/her potential and reach national and even international levels of competition?

   d) The National Coaching Foundation co-ordinates coaching for all user groups. Describe THREE of these initiatives designed to improve coaching and support for performers.

      i)

      ii)

      iii)

2. With reference to one particular sport, describe how a person may progress from 'grass roots' level to 'elite' performer!

1. Complete the following crossword using the clues below. Use page 81 of your Revision Guide to help you.

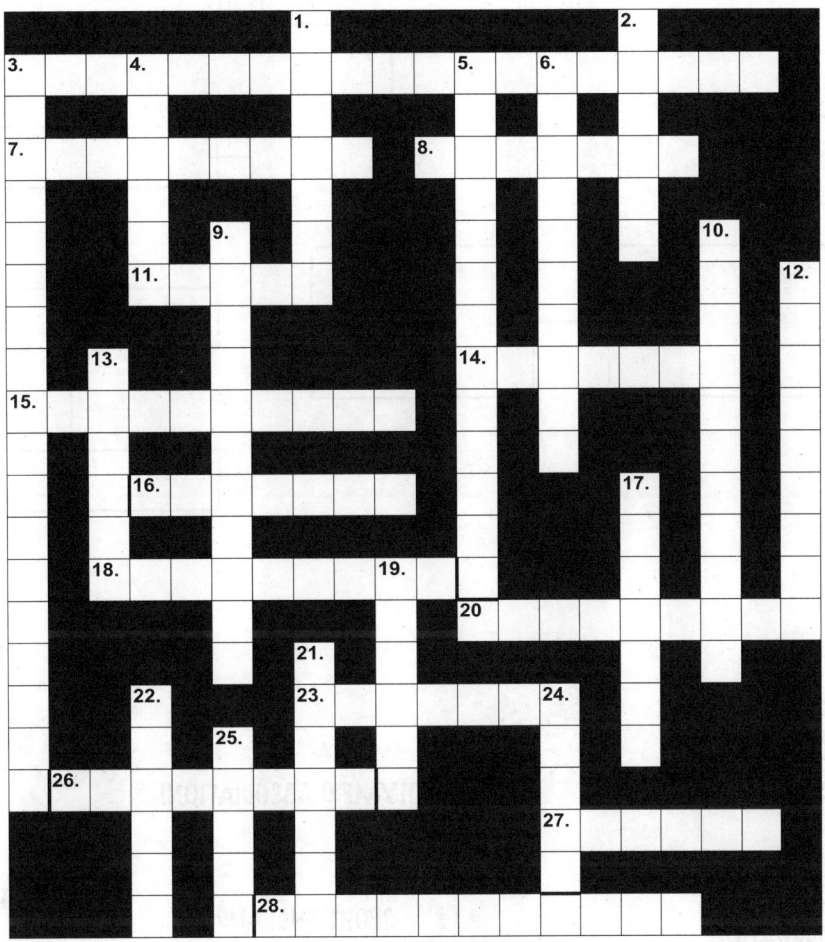

ACROSS:
3. Also called National Sports Centres (7, 2, 10).
7. Track events at the Olympics for example (9).
8. Riding a bicycle (7).
11. In some sports individuals compete, in others .... compete (5).
14. They might play tennis, football or rugby for example (7).
15. Sports people might also be called p .... (10).
16. See 12 DOWN.
18. A foundation which develops excellence and encourages talent (6, 3).
20. Unrealised capability is sometimes called p .... (9).
23. To teach or instruct (7).
26. They are often thought of as a minority group (8).
27. The number of National Sports Centres in the U.K. (6).
28. A way of raising money (11).

DOWN:
1. Teaches and trains (7).
2. Wimbledon is famous for it (6).
3. Specially designed training regimes (8, 10).
4. A natural ability for something (6).
5. The Centre of Excellence for athletics is here (7, 6).
6. The Centre of Excellence for football is here (10).
9. Water skiing and windsurfing are common examples (5, 6).
10. A centre for outdoor pursuits (4, 1, 6).
12. and 16 ACROSS. In many cases parents and families provide .... (9, 7).
13. Subsidies from Governing bodies (6).
17. See 19 DOWN.
19. and 17 DOWN. Provided by Centres of Excellence to treat muscle strains, for example (6, 7).
21. If we promote and cultivate excellence we d .... it (7).
22. and 25. Tennis facilities are provided here (6, 5)
24. Select few (5).
25. See 22 DOWN.

1. Complete the framework below using the names of the sports organisations given.

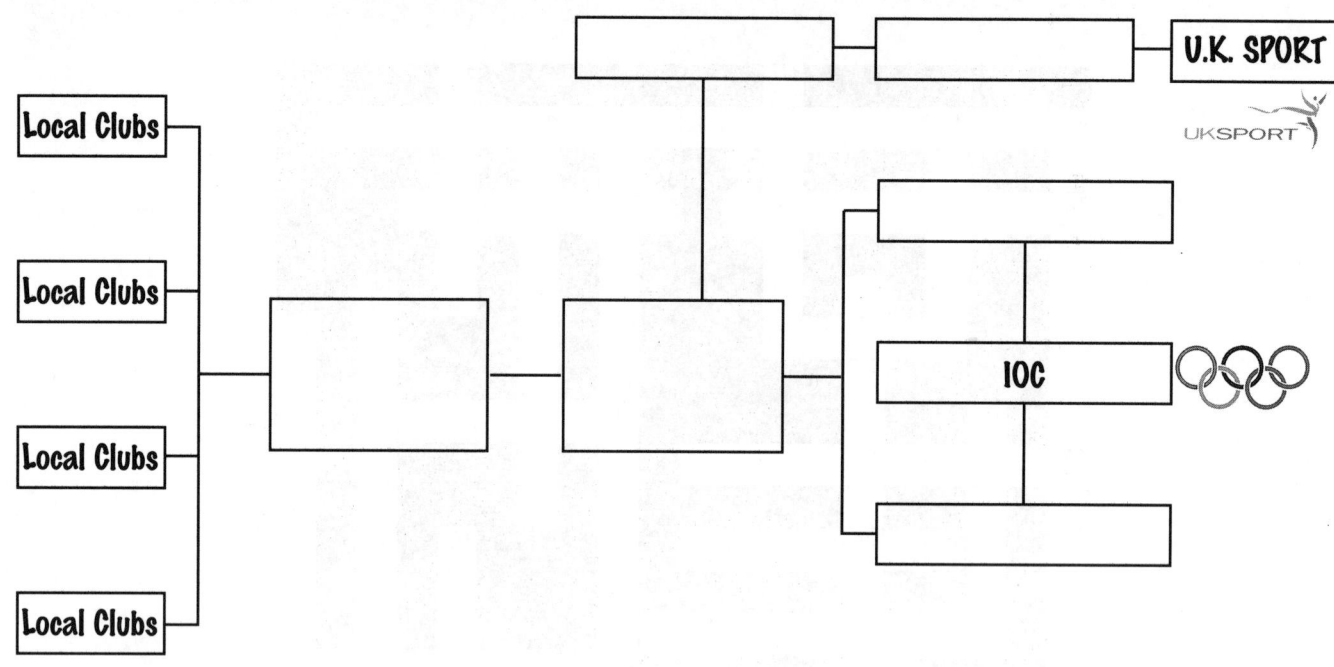

Local Clubs

Local Clubs

Local Clubs

Local Clubs

U.K. SPORT

UKSPORT

IOC

C.C.P.R. (CENTRAL COUNCIL FOR PHYSICAL RECREATION)

B.O.A. (BRITISH OLYMPIC ASSOCIATION)

 LTA NATIONAL GOVERNING BODIES

INTERNATIONAL SPORTS FEDERATION

 SPORT ENGLAND

REGIONAL GOVERNING BODIES

2. The National Governing Body of a sport has many important functions, such as encouraging participation at all levels.

a) List FIVE other duties or responsibilities with a brief explanation of each.

i) ....

ii) ....

iii) ....

iv) ....

v) ....

b) How might a National Governing Body encourage people of all ages and abilities to participate in its sport?

1. U.K. SPORT has responsibility for sport in the U.K. as a whole, whilst each Home Country has its own sports council e.g. SPORT ENGLAND.

a) What are the KEY ROLES of U.K. SPORT?

UKSPORT

b) What are the KEY ROLES of the HOME COUNTRY COUNCILS e.g. SPORT ENGLAND?

SPORT ENGLAND

2. The CENTRAL COUNCIL FOR PHYSICAL RECREATION is an umbrella C.C.P.R. organisation with more than 300 members.

a) Which sporting organisations make up the membership of the CCPR?

CC PR

b) The CCPR has six subdivisions and members can belong to one or more. Name FOUR of them.

i)

ii)

iii)

iv)

c) What are the KEY ROLES of the CCPR?

1. The International Olympic Committee (IOC) is a very powerful organisation, with total responsibility for the Olympic Games.

a) Which people, from which organisations, make up the IOC?

....

b) What are the KEY ROLES of the IOC?

....
....
....
....
....

2. The BRITISH OLYMPIC ASSOCIATION (BOA) is responsible for all events connected with the Olympic Games in Great Britain.

a) One of its KEY ROLES is to raise money without political involvement. List FOUR others.

i) ....

ii) ....

iii) ....

iv) ....

b) How does the BOA raise money?

....
....

3. Not all organisations that influence participation are directly involved in sport. The Countryside Agency is responsible for the English Countryside.

The Countryside Agency

Name THREE English National Parks and the Countryside Agency's role in maintaining them.

i) .... ii) .... iii) ....

The Countryside Agency maintains the National Park by ...

i) ....

ii) ....

iii) ....